Jack and Jill
Student Workbook | Part 2

SpellingYouSee™
Building Confidence

A Demme Learning Publication

Jack and Jill Student Workbook, Parts 1 and 2
©2014 Spelling You See
©2012 Karen J. Holinga, PhD.
Published and distributed by Demme Learning

www.SpellingYouSee.com

1-888-854-6284 or +1 717-283-1448 | www.demmelearning.com
Lancaster, Pennsylvania USA

ISBN 978-1-60826-603-6 (Jack and Jill Student Workbook)
ISBN 978-1-60826-605-0 (Part 2)
Revision Code 0816

Printed in the United States of America by Bindery Associates LLC

For information regarding CPSIA on this printed material call: 1-888-854-6284
and provide reference #0616-07272016

To the Instructor

This student book is the second half of Level B of Spelling You See, an innovative spelling program designed to help your student become a confident and successful speller. These lessons provide more practice with the letter patterns introduced in *Jack and Jill Student Workbook, Part 1*. This is a good time to review the instructions and tips in your *Instructor's Handbook*.

1. Read the rhyme with your student. Say it together and clap in rhythm.

2. Read it together slowly. Have the student point to each word as you read.

3. A vowel chunk is two vowels that usually make one sound. Work with your student to find all the **vowel chunks** in the passage and mark them using a yellow pencil or highlighter. Not all the chunks in the box will occur in the passage.

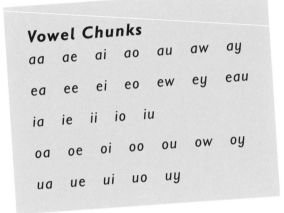

Vowel Chunks

aa	ae	ai	ao	au	aw	ay
ea	ee	ei	eo	ew	ey	eau
ia	ie	ii	io	iu		
oa	oe	oi	oo	ou	ow	oy
ua	ue	ui	uo	uy		

I'm a little teapot,

Short and stout.

Here is my handle,

Here is my spout.

When I get all steamed up,

Hear me shout.

Then tip me over

And pour me out!

Jack and Jill

Copy and "chunk" the passage on the lines below. You may look at the opposite page if you need help marking the vowel chunks.

I'm a little teapot,

I'm

Short and stout.

Short

Here is my handle,

Here

Here is my spout.

Here

1. Read the rhyme with your student. Say it together and clap in rhythm.

2. Read it together slowly. Have the student point to each word as you read.

3. Work with your student to find all the **vowel chunks** and mark them in yellow.

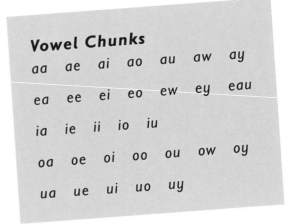

Vowel Chunks

aa	ae	ai	ao	au	aw	ay
ea	ee	ei	eo	ew	ey	eau
ia	ie	ii	io	iu		
oa	oe	oi	oo	ou	ow	oy
ua	ue	ui	uo	uy		

I'm a little teapot,

Short and stout.

Here is my handle,

Here is my spout.

When I get all steamed up,

Hear me shout.

Then tip me over

And pour me out!

Jack and Jill

Copy and "chunk" the passage on the lines below. You may look at the opposite page if you need help marking the vowel chunks.

When I get all steamed up,

W

Hear me shout.

H

Then tip me over

T

And pour me out!

A

1. Read the rhyme with your student. Say it together and clap in rhythm.

2. Read it together slowly. Have the student point to each word as you read.

3. Together, find all the **vowel chunks** in the passage and mark them in yellow.

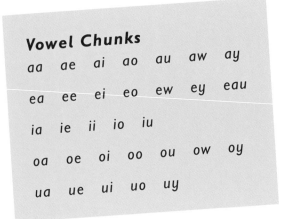

Vowel Chunks

aa	ae	ai	ao	au	aw	ay
ea	ee	ei	eo	ew	ey	eau
ia	ie	ii	io	iu		
oa	oe	oi	oo	ou	ow	oy
ua	ue	ui	uo	uy		

I'm a little teapot,

Short and stout.

Here is my handle,

Here is my spout.

When I get all steamed up,

Hear me shout.

Then tip me over

And pour me out!

Copy and "chunk" the passage on the lines below. You may look at the opposite page if you need help marking the vowel chunks.

I'm a little teapot,

I

Short and stout.

S

Here is my handle,

H

Here is my spout.

H

19D

1. Read the rhyme with your student. Say it together and clap in rhythm.

2. Read it together slowly. Have the student point to each word as you read.

3. Together, find all the <u>vowel chunks</u> in the passage and mark them in yellow.

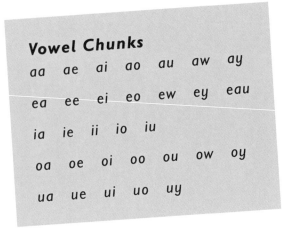

Vowel Chunks

aa	ae	ai	ao	au	aw	ay
ea	ee	ei	eo	ew	ey	eau
ia	ie	ii	io	iu		
oa	oe	oi	oo	ou	ow	oy
ua	ue	ui	uo	uy		

I'm a little teapot,

Short and stout.

Here is my handle,

Here is my spout.

When I get all steamed up,

Hear me shout.

Then tip me over

And pour me out!

Jack and Jill

Draw a picture of the rhyme or write your own story. Be creative and have fun.

1. Read the rhyme with your student. Say it together and clap in rhythm.

2. Read it together slowly. Have the student point to each word as you read.

3. Together, find all the **vowel chunks** in the passage and mark them in yellow.

4. All the rhymes in this workbook are also in the back of the *Instructor's Handbook* under **Resources**. When dictating the passage, you may want to cover this page with a piece of paper and read the rhyme from the *Handbook*.

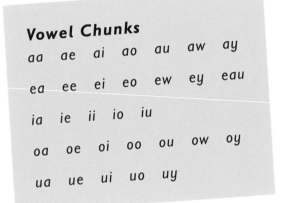

Vowel Chunks

aa	ae	ai	ao	au	aw	ay
ea	ee	ei	eo	ew	ey	eau
ia	ie	ii	io	iu		
oa	oe	oi	oo	ou	ow	oy
ua	ue	ui	uo	uy		

I'm a little teapot,

Short and stout.

Here is my handle,

Here is my spout.

When I get all steamed up,

Hear me shout.

Then tip me over

And pour me out!

Jack and Jill

Write this week's rhyme from dictation. Take your time. Ask for help if you need it.

I'm

Short

Here

Here

When

Hear

Then

And

I spelled _____ words correctly.

Section 1: Vowel Chunks, Silent Letters

1. Read the rhyme with your student. Say it together and clap in rhythm.

2. Read it together slowly. Have the student point to each word as you read.

3. Help your student find all the **vowel chunks** in the passage and mark them with yellow. Together, look for any **silent _e_** that is not part of a vowel chunk and mark it in orange.

Little Bo Peep has lost her sheep

And doesn't know where to find them.

Leave them alone, and they'll come home,

Wagging their tails behind them.

Vowel Chunks

aa	ae	ai	ao	au	aw	ay
ea	ee	ei	eo	ew	ey	eau
ia	ie	ii	io	iu		
oa	oe	oi	oo	ou	ow	oy
ua	ue	ui	uo	uy		

Copy and "chunk" the passage on the lines below. Mark the vowel chunks and each silent *e*.

Little Bo Peep

Little

has lost her sheep

has

And doesn't know

And

where to find them.

where

20B

Section 1: Vowel Chunks, Silent Letters

1. Read the rhyme with your student. Say it together and clap in rhythm.

2. Read it together slowly. Have the student point to each word as you read.

3. Together, mark the <u>**vowel chunks**</u> with yellow and each **silent _e_** in orange.

Little Bo Peep has lost her sheep

And doesn't know where to find them.

Leave them alone, and they'll come home,

Wagging their tails behind them.

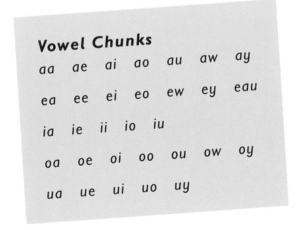

Vowel Chunks

aa	ae	ai	ao	au	aw	ay
ea	ee	ei	eo	ew	ey	eau
ia	ie	ii	io	iu		
oa	oe	oi	oo	ou	ow	oy
ua	ue	ui	uo	uy		

Jack and Jill

Copy and "chunk" the passage on the lines below. Mark the vowel chunks and each silent *e*.

Leave   them   alone,

L

and   they'll   come   home,

a

Wagging   their   tails

W

behind   them.

b

1. Read the rhyme with your student. Say it together and clap in rhythm.

2. Read it together slowly. Have the student point to each word as you read.

3. Together, mark the **vowel chunks** with yellow and each **silent _e_** in orange.

Little Bo Peep has lost her sheep

And doesn't know where to find them.

Leave them alone, and they'll come home,

Wagging their tails behind them.

Vowel Chunks

aa	ae	ai	ao	au	aw	ay
ea	ee	ei	eo	ew	ey	eau
ia	ie	ii	io	iu		
oa	oe	oi	oo	ou	ow	oy
ua	ue	ui	uo	uy		

Copy and "chunk" the passage on the lines below. Mark the vowel chunks and each silent *e*.

Little   Bo   Peep

L

has   lost   her   sheep

h

And   doesn't   know

A

where   to   find   them.

W

Section 1: Vowel Chunks, Silent Letters

1. Read the rhyme with your student. Say it together and clap in rhythm.

2. Read it together slowly. Have the student point to each word as you read.

3. Together, mark the <u>vowel chunks</u> with yellow and each **silent _e_** in orange.

Little Bo Peep has lost her sheep

And doesn't know where to find them.

Leave them alone, and they'll come home,

Wagging their tails behind them.

Vowel Chunks

aa	ae	ai	ao	au	aw	ay
ea	ee	ei	eo	ew	ey	eau
ia	ie	ii	io	iu		
oa	oe	oi	oo	ou	ow	oy
ua	ue	ui	uo	uy		

Draw a picture of the rhyme or write your own story. Be creative and have fun.

1. Read the rhyme with your student. Say it together and clap in rhythm.

2. Read it together slowly. Have the student point to each word as you read.

3. Together, mark the **vowel chunks** with yellow and each **silent _e_** in orange.

Little Bo Peep has lost her sheep

And doesn't know where to find them.

Leave them alone, and they'll come home,

Wagging their tails behind them.

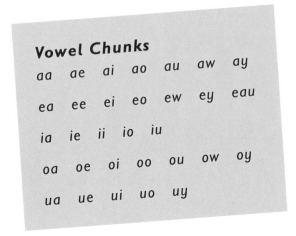

Vowel Chunks

aa ae ai ao au aw ay

ea ee ei eo ew ey eau

ia ie ii io iu

oa oe oi oo ou ow oy

ua ue ui uo uy

Write this week's rhyme from dictation. Take your time. Ask for help if you need it.

Little

has

And

where

Leave

and

Wagging

behind

I spelled _____ words correctly.

1. Read the rhyme with your student. Say it together and clap in rhythm.

2. Read it together slowly. Have the student point to each word as you read.

3. Together, look for **vowel chunks** and mark them in yellow. Mark each **Tricky y Guy** in green.

The itsy, bitsy spider went up the water spout.

Down came the rain and washed the spider out.

Out came the sun and dried up all the rain,

And the itsy, bitsy spider went up the spout again.

Vowel Chunks

aa ae ai ao au aw ay

ea ee ei eo ew ey eau

ia ie ii io iu

oa oe oi oo ou ow oy

ua ue ui uo uy

Copy and "chunk" the passage. Mark the vowel chunks and each Tricky *y* Guy.

The itsy, bitsy spider

The

went up the water spout.

went

Down came the rain and

Down

washed the spider out.

washed

1. Read the rhyme with your student. Say it together and clap in rhythm.

2. Read it together slowly. Have the student point to each word as you read.

3. Together, look for **vowel chunks** and mark them in yellow. Mark each **Tricky *y* Guy** in green.

The itsy, bitsy spider went up the water spout.

Down came the rain and washed the spider out.

Out came the sun and dried up all the rain,

And the itsy, bitsy spider went up the spout again.

Vowel Chunks

aa   ae   ai   ao   au   aw   ay

ea   ee   ei   eo   ew   ey   eau

ia   ie   ii   io   iu

oa   oe   oi   oo   ou   ow   oy

ua   ue   ui   uo   uy

Copy and "chunk" the passage. Mark the vowel chunks and each Tricky *y* Guy.

Out came the sun and

O

dried up all the rain,

d

And the itsy, bitsy spider

A

went up the spout again.

W

1. Read the rhyme with your student. Say it together and clap in rhythm.

2. Read it together slowly. Have the student point to each word as you read.

3. Together, look for **vowel chunks** and mark them in yellow. Mark each **Tricky *y* Guy** in green.

The itsy, bitsy spider went up the water spout.

Down came the rain and washed the spider out.

Out came the sun and dried up all the rain,

And the itsy, bitsy spider went up the spout again.

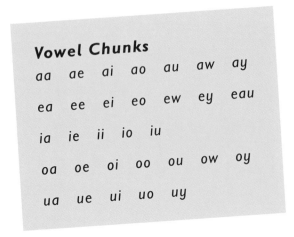

Vowel Chunks

aa ae ai ao au aw ay

ea ee ei eo ew ey eau

ia ie ii io iu

oa oe oi oo ou ow oy

ua ue ui uo uy

Copy and "chunk" the passage. Mark the vowel chunks and each Tricky *y* Guy.

The itsy, bitsy spider

T

went up the water spout.

W

Down came the rain and

D

washed the spider out.

W

1. Read the rhyme with your student. Say it together and clap in rhythm.

2. Read it together slowly. Have the student point to each word as you read.

3. Together, look for **vowel chunks** and mark them in yellow. Mark each **Tricky *y* Guy** in green.

The itsy, bitsy spider went up the water spout.

Down came the rain and washed the spider out.

Out came the sun and dried up all the rain,

And the itsy, bitsy spider went up the spout again.

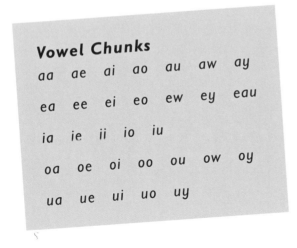

Vowel Chunks

aa ae ai ao au aw ay

ea ee ei eo ew ey eau

ia ie ii io iu

oa oe oi oo ou ow oy

ua ue ui uo uy

Section 2: No Rule Day

Draw a picture of the rhyme or write your own story. Be creative and have fun.

1. Read the rhyme with your student. Say it together and clap in rhythm.

2. Read it together slowly. Have the student point to each word as you read.

3. Together, look for **vowel chunks** and mark them in yellow. Mark each **Tricky y Guy** in green.

The itsy, bitsy spider went up the water spout.

Down came the rain and washed the spider out.

Out came the sun and dried up all the rain,

And the itsy, bitsy spider went up the spout again.

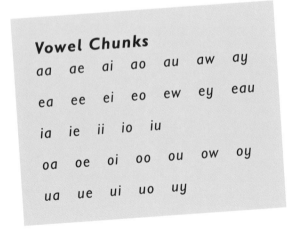

Vowel Chunks

aa ae ai ao au aw ay

ea ee ei eo ew ey eau

ia ie ii io iu

oa oe oi oo ou ow oy

ua ue ui uo uy

Section 2: Dictation

Write this week's rhyme from dictation. Take your time. Ask for help if you need it.

The

Down

Out

And

I spelled ______ words correctly.

1. Read the rhyme to your student.

2. Read it together slowly. Have the student point to each word as you read.

3. Together, look for **Bossy *r* chunks** and mark them in purple.

Bossy r Chunks
ar er ir or ur

Old Mother Hubbard

Went to her cupboard

To get her poor dog a bone.

But when she got there,

Her cupboard was bare,

And so the poor dog had none.

Copy the passage. Mark the Bossy *r* chunks.

Old Mother Hubbard

Old

Went to her cupboard

Went

To get her poor dog

To

a bone.

a

1. Read the rhyme to your student.

2. Read it together slowly. Have the student point to each word as you read.

3. Together, look for **Bossy *r* chunks** and mark them in purple.

Old Mother Hubbard

Went to her cupboard

To get her poor dog a bone.

But when she got there,

Her cupboard was bare,

And so the poor dog had none.

Bossy r Chunks
ar   er   ir   or   ur

Copy the passage. Mark the Bossy *r* chunks.

But when she got there,

B

Her cupboard was bare,

H

And so the poor dog

A

had none.

h

1. Read the rhyme to your student.

2. Read it together slowly. Have the student point to each word as you read.

3. Together, look for **Bossy *r* chunks** and mark them in purple.

Bossy r Chunks
ar   er   ir   or   ur

Old Mother Hubbard

Went to her cupboard

To get her poor dog a bone.

But when she got there,

Her cupboard was bare,

And so the poor dog had none.

Copy the passage. Mark the Bossy *r* chunks.

Old Mother Hubbard

O

Went to her cupboard

W

To get her poor dog

T

a bone.

a

1. Read the rhyme to your student.

2. Read it together slowly. Have the student point to each word as you read.

3. Together, look for **Bossy *r* chunks** and mark them in purple.

Old Mother Hubbard

Went to her cupboard

To get her poor dog a bone.

But when she got there,

Her cupboard was bare,

And so the poor dog had none.

Draw a picture of the rhyme or write your own story. Be creative and have fun.

1. Read the rhyme to your student.

2. Read it together slowly. Have the student point to each word as you read.

3. Together, look for **Bossy *r* chunks** and mark them in purple.

Bossy r Chunks
ar   er   ir   or   ur

Old Mother Hubbard

Went to her cupboard

To get her poor dog a bone.

But when she got there,

Her cupboard was bare,

And so the poor dog had none.

Write this week's rhyme from dictation. Take your time. Ask for help if you need it.

Old

Went

To

But

Her

And

I spelled _____ words correctly.

1. Read the rhyme to your student.

2. Read it together slowly. Have the student point to each word as you read.

3. Together, look for all the **vowel chunks** in the passage and mark them in yellow.

Tom, he was a piper's son.

He learned to play when he was young,

But the only tune that he could play

Was "Over the Hills and Far Away."

Vowel Chunks

aa	ae	ai	ao	au	aw	ay
ea	ee	ei	eo	ew	ey	eau
ia	ie	ii	io	iu		
oa	oe	oi	oo	ou	ow	oy
ua	ue	ui	uo	uy		

Copy the passage and mark the vowel chunks.

Tom, he was

Tom

a piper's son.

a

He learned to play

He

when he was young,

when

23B

Section 1: Vowel Chunks

1. Read the rhyme to your student.

2. Read it together slowly. Have the student point to each word as you read.

3. Together, look for all the **vowel chunks** in the passage and mark them in yellow.

Tom, he was a piper's son.

He learned to play when he was young,

But the only tune that he could play

Was "Over the Hills and Far Away."

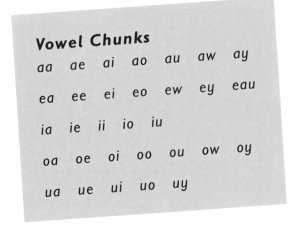

Vowel Chunks

aa	ae	ai	ao	au	aw	ay
ea	ee	ei	eo	ew	ey	eau
ia	ie	ii	io	iu		
oa	oe	oi	oo	ou	ow	oy
ua	ue	ui	uo	uy		

46

Jack and Jill

Copy the passage and mark the vowel chunks.

But the only tune

that he could play

Was "Over the Hills

and Far Away."

23C

Section 1: Vowel Chunks

1. Read the rhyme to your student.

2. Read it together slowly. Have the student point to each word as you read.

3. Together, look for all the **vowel chunks** in the passage and mark them in yellow.

Tom, he was a piper's son.

He learned to play when he was young,

But the only tune that he could play

Was "Over the Hills and Far Away."

Vowel Chunks

aa	ae	ai	ao	au	aw	ay
ea	ee	ei	eo	ew	ey	eau
ia	ie	ii	io	iu		
oa	oe	oi	oo	ou	ow	oy
ua	ue	ui	uo	uy		

48

Jack and Jill

Section 2: Copywork

Copy the passage and mark the vowel chunks.

Tom, he was

T

a piper's son.

a

He learned to play

H

when he was young,

W

1. Read the rhyme to your student.

2. Read it together slowly. Have the student point to each word as you read.

3. Together, look for all the **vowel chunks** in the passage and mark them in yellow.

Tom, he was a piper's son.

He learned to play when he was young,

But the only tune that he could play

Was "Over the Hills and Far Away."

Vowel Chunks

aa	ae	ai	ao	au	aw	ay
ea	ee	ei	eo	ew	ey	eau
ia	ie	ii	io	iu		
oa	oe	oi	oo	ou	ow	oy
ua	ue	ui	uo	uy		

Draw a picture of the rhyme or write your own story. Be creative and have fun.

1. Read the rhyme to your student.

2. Read it together slowly. Have the student point to each word as you read.

3. Together, look for all the **vowel chunks** in the passage and mark them in yellow.

Tom, he was a piper's son.

He learned to play when he was young,

But the only tune that he could play

Was "Over the Hills and Far Away."

Vowel Chunks

aa   ae   ai   ao   au   aw   ay

ea   ee   ei   eo   ew   ey   eau

ia   ie   ii   io   iu

oa   oe   oi   oo   ou   ow   oy

ua   ue   ui   uo   uy

Write this week's rhyme from dictation. Take your time. Ask for help if you need it.

Tom

He

But

Was

I spelled _____ words correctly.

1. Read the rhyme to your student.

2. Read it together slowly. Have the student point to each word as you read.

3. This week, you and your student will mark both **vowel chunks** and **Bossy *r* chunks**. Remember to use yellow for vowel chunks and purple for Bossy *r* chunks.

Roses are red.

Violets are blue.

Sugar is sweet,

And so are you.

Vowel Chunks

aa	ae	ai	ao	au	aw	ay
ea	ee	ei	eo	ew	ey	eau
ia	ie	ii	io	iu		
oa	oe	oi	oo	ou	ow	oy
ua	ue	ui	uo	uy		

Bossy r Chunks

ar   er   ir   or   ur

Section 2: Copywork

Copy the passage and mark the vowel chunks and Bossy *r* chunks.

Roses are red.
Roses

Violets are blue.
Violets

Sugar is sweet,
Sugar

And so are you.
And

Jack and Jill 24A

1. Read the rhyme to your student.

2. Read it together slowly. Have the student point to each word as you read.

3. Together, mark both **vowel chunks** and **Bossy *r* chunks**. Remember to use yellow for vowel chunks and purple for Bossy *r* chunks.

Roses are red.

Violets are blue.

Sugar is sweet,

And so are you.

Vowel Chunks

aa ae ai ao au aw ay

ea ee ei eo ew ey eau

ia ie ii io iu

oa oe oi oo ou ow oy

ua ue ui uo uy

Bossy r Chunks

ar er ir or ur

Copy the passage and mark the vowel chunks and Bossy *r* chunks.

Roses are red.

R

Violets are blue.

V

Sugar is sweet,

S

And so are you.

A

1. Read the rhyme to your student.

2. Read it together slowly. Have the student point to each word as you read.

3. Together, mark both **vowel chunks** and **Bossy *r* chunks**. Remember to use yellow for vowel chunks and purple for Bossy *r* chunks.

Roses are red.

Violets are blue.

Sugar is sweet,

And so are you.

Vowel Chunks

aa   ae   ai   ao   au   aw   ay

ea   ee   ei   eo   ew   ey   eau

ia   ie   ii   io   iu

oa   oe   oi   oo   ou   ow   oy

ua   ue   ui   uo   uy

Bossy r Chunks

ar   er   ir   or   ur

Copy the passage and mark the vowel chunks and Bossy *r* chunks.

Roses are red.

R

Violets are blue.

V

Sugar is sweet,

S

And so are you.

A

1. Read the rhyme to your student.

2. Read it together slowly. Have the student point to each word as you read.

3. Together, mark both <u>**vowel chunks**</u> and <u>**Bossy *r* chunks**</u>. Remember to use yellow for vowel chunks and purple for Bossy *r* chunks.

Roses are red.

Violets are blue.

Sugar is sweet,

And so are you.

Vowel Chunks

aa	ae	ai	ao	au	aw	ay
ea	ee	ei	eo	ew	ey	eau
ia	ie	ii	io	iu		
oa	oe	oi	oo	ou	ow	oy
ua	ue	ui	uo	uy		

Bossy r Chunks

ar   er   ir   or   ur

Draw a picture of the rhyme or write your own story. Be creative and have fun.

24E

1. Read the rhyme to your student.

2. Read it together slowly. Have the student point to each word as you read.

3. Together, mark both **vowel chunks** and **Bossy *r* chunks**. Remember to use yellow for vowel chunks and purple for Bossy *r* chunks.

Roses are red.

Violets are blue.

Sugar is sweet,

And so are you.

Vowel Chunks

aa	ae	ai	ao	au	aw	ay
ea	ee	ei	eo	ew	ey	eau
ia	ie	ii	io	iu		
oa	oe	oi	oo	ou	ow	oy
ua	ue	ui	uo	uy		

Bossy r Chunks

ar   er   ir   or   ur

Jack and Jill

Section 2: Dictation

Write this week's rhyme from dictation. Take your time. Ask for help if you need it.

Roses

Violets

Sugar

And

I spelled _____ words correctly.

1. Read the rhyme to your student.

2. Read it together slowly. Have the student point to each word as you read.

3. Have your student mark **vowel chunks** in yellow and **Bossy *r* chunks** in purple. Be prepared to give as much help as is needed.

Little Boy Blue,

Come blow your horn.

The sheep's in the meadow.

The cow's in the corn.

But where is the little boy

Who looks after the sheep?

He's under the haystack, fast asleep!

Bossy r Chunks

ar   er   ir   or   ur

Vowel Chunks

aa	ae	ai	ao	au	aw	ay
ea	ee	ei	eo	ew	ey	eau
ia	ie	ii	io	iu		
oa	oe	oi	oo	ou	ow	oy
ua	ue	ui	uo	uy		

Copy the passage and mark the vowel chunks and Bossy *r* chunks.

Little   Boy   Blue,

Little

Come   blow   your   horn.

Come

The   sheep's   in   the   meadow.

The

The   cow's   in   the   corn.

The

25B
Section 1: Vowel Chunks, Bossy *r* Chunks

1. Read the rhyme to your student.

2. Read it together slowly. Have the student point to each word as you read.

3. Have your student mark **vowel chunks** in yellow and **Bossy *r* chunks** in purple. Be prepared to give as much help as is needed.

Little Boy Blue,

Come blow your horn.

The sheep's in the meadow.

The cow's in the corn.

But where is the little boy

Who looks after the sheep?

He's under the haystack, fast asleep!

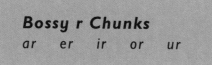

Bossy r Chunks
ar   er   ir   or   ur

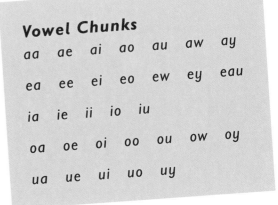

Vowel Chunks
aa   ae   ai   ao   au   aw   ay

ea   ee   ei   eo   ew   ey   eau

ia   ie   ii   io   iu

oa   oe   oi   oo   ou   ow   oy

ua   ue   ui   uo   uy

Jack and Jill

Copy the passage and mark the vowel chunks and Bossy *r* chunks.

But where is the little boy

B

Who looks after the sheep?

W

He's under the haystack,

H

fast asleep!

f

Jack and Jill   25B

1. Read the rhyme to your student.

2. Read it together slowly. Have the student point to each word as you read.

3. Have your student mark <u>**vowel chunks**</u> in yellow and <u>**Bossy r chunks**</u> in purple. Be prepared to give as much help as is needed.

Little Boy Blue,

Come blow your horn.

The sheep's in the meadow.

The cow's in the corn.

But where is the little boy

Who looks after the sheep?

He's under the haystack, fast asleep!

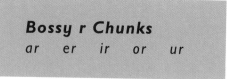

Bossy r Chunks

ar   er   ir   or   ur

Vowel Chunks

aa ae ai ao au aw ay

ea ee ei eo ew ey eau

ia ie ii io iu

oa oe oi oo ou ow oy

ua ue ui uo uy

Copy the passage and mark the vowel chunks and Bossy *r* chunks.

Little   Boy   Blue,

Come   blow   your   horn.

The   sheep's   in   the   meadow.

The   cow's   in   the   corn.

1. Read the rhyme to your student.

2. Read it together slowly. Have the student point to each word as you read.

3. Have your student mark **vowel chunks** in yellow and **Bossy *r* chunks** in purple. Be prepared to give as much help as is needed.

Little Boy Blue,

Come blow your horn.

The sheep's in the meadow.

The cow's in the corn.

But where is the little boy

Who looks after the sheep?

He's under the haystack, fast asleep!

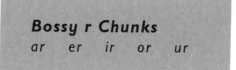

Bossy r Chunks

ar   er   ir   or   ur

Vowel Chunks

aa   ae   ai   ao   au   aw   ay

ea   ee   ei   eo   ew   ey   eau

ia   ie   ii   io   iu

oa   oe   oi   oo   ou   ow   oy

ua   ue   ui   uo   uy

Draw a picture of the rhyme or write your own story. Be creative and have fun.

Section 1: Vowel Chunks, Bossy *r* Chunks

1. Read the rhyme to your student.

2. Read it together slowly. Have the student point to each word as you read.

3. Have your student mark **vowel chunks** in yellow and **Bossy *r* chunks** in purple. Be prepared to give as much help as is needed.

Little Boy Blue,

Come blow your horn.

The sheep's in the meadow.

The cow's in the corn.

But where is the little boy

Who looks after the sheep?

He's under the haystack, fast asleep!

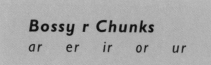

Bossy r Chunks

ar   er   ir   or   ur

Vowel Chunks

aa   ae   ai   ao   au   aw   ay

ea   ee   ei   eo   ew   ey   eau

ia   ie   ii   io   iu

oa   oe   oi   oo   ou   ow   oy

ua   ue   ui   uo   uy

Write this week's rhyme from dictation. Take your time. Ask for help if you need it.

Little

Come

The

The

But

Who

He's

I spelled _____ words correctly.

Section 1: Consonant Chunks

1. Read the rhyme to your student.

2. Read it together slowly. Have the student point to each word as you read.

3. Help your student look for and mark all the **consonant chunks** in blue. Notice that some consonant chunks may be silent. An example is *gh* in the word *light*.

Star light, star bright,

First star I see tonight,

I wish I may, I wish I might

Have the wish I wish tonight.

Consonant Chunks

ch	gh	ph	sh	th	wh		
gn	kn	qu	wr	dg	ck	tch	
bb	cc	dd	ff	gg	hh	kk	ll	mm
nn	pp	rr	ss	tt	ww	vv	zz	

Jack and Jill

Copy the passage and mark all the consonant chunks.

Star light, star bright,

Star

First star I see tonight,

First

I wish I may,

I

I wish I might

I

1. Read the rhyme to your student.

2. Read it together slowly. Have the student point to each word as you read.

3. Help your student look for and mark all the **consonant chunks** in blue. A consonant chunk may make a new sound, or the letters may be silent.

Star light, star bright,

First star I see tonight,

I wish I may, I wish I might

Have the wish I wish tonight.

Consonant Chunks

ch	gh	ph	sh	th	wh	
gn	kn	qu	wr	dg	ck	tch
bb	cc	dd	ff	gg	hh	kk	ll	mm
nn	pp	rr	ss	tt	ww	vv	zz

Copy the passage and mark all the consonant chunks.

I wish I may,

I wish I might

Have the wish

I wish tonight.

1. Read the rhyme to your student.

2. Read it together slowly. Have the student point to each word as you read.

3. Help your student look for and mark all the **consonant chunks** in blue. A consonant chunk may make a new sound, or the letters may be silent.

Star light, star bright,

First star I see tonight,

I wish I may, I wish I might

Have the wish I wish tonight.

Consonant Chunks

ch	gh	ph	sh	th	wh		
gn	kn	qu	wr	dg	ck	tch	
bb	cc	dd	ff	gg	hh	kk	ll	mm
nn	pp	rr	ss	tt	ww	vv	zz

Copy the passage and mark all the consonant chunks.

Star light, star bright,

S

First star I see tonight,

F

I

I wish I may,

I

I wish I might

I

26D

Section 1: Consonant Chunks

1. Read the rhyme to your student.

2. Read it together slowly. Have the student point to each word as you read.

3. Help your student look for and mark all the **consonant chunks** in blue. A consonant chunk may make a new sound, or the letters may be silent.

Star light, star bright,

First star I see tonight,

I wish I may, I wish I might

Have the wish I wish tonight.

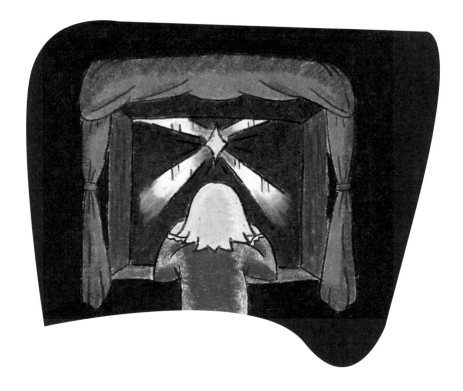

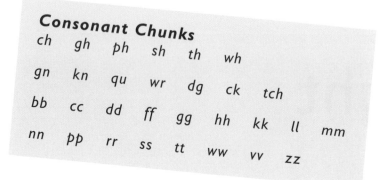

Consonant Chunks

ch	gh	ph	sh	th	wh
gn	kn	qu	wr	dg	ck	tch
bb	cc	dd	ff	gg	hh	kk	ll	mm
nn	pp	rr	ss	tt	ww	vv	zz

80

Jack and Jill

Draw a picture of the rhyme or write your own story. Be creative and have fun.

1. Read the rhyme to your student.

2. Read it together slowly. Have the student point to each word as you read.

3. Help your student look for and mark all the **consonant chunks** in blue. A consonant chunk may make a new sound, or the letters may be silent.

Star light, star bright,

First star I see tonight,

I wish I may, I wish I might

Have the wish I wish tonight.

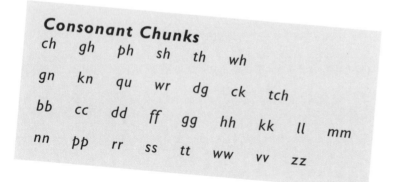

Consonant Chunks

ch gh ph sh th wh

gn kn qu wr dg ck tch

bb cc dd ff gg hh kk ll mm

nn pp rr ss tt ww vv zz

Write this week's rhyme from dictation. Take your time. Ask for help if you need it.

Star

First

I

I

Have

I

I spelled _____ words correctly.   **83**

1. Read the rhyme to your student.

2. Read it together slowly. Have the student point to each word as you read.

3. Have your student look for and mark all the **consonant chunks** in blue. Continue to give as much help as is needed.

There once was a jolly miller

Who lived on the river Dee.

He worked and sang from morn till night,

No lark more happy than he.

Consonant Chunks

ch	gh	ph	sh	th	wh				
gn	kn	qu	wr	dg	ck	tch			
bb	cc	dd	ff	gg	hh	kk	ll	mm	
nn	pp	rr	ss	tt	ww	vv	zz		

Copy the passage and mark all the consonant chunks.

There   once   was

There

a   jolly   miller

a

Who   lived   on

Who

the   river   Dee.

the

27B

1. Read the rhyme to your student.

2. Read it together slowly. Have the student point to each word as you read.

3. Have your student look for and mark all the <u>**consonant chunks**</u> in blue. Continue to give as much help as is needed.

There once was a jolly miller

Who lived on the river Dee.

He worked and sang from morn till night,

No lark more happy than he.

Consonant Chunks

ch	gh	ph	sh	th	wh			
gn	kn	qu	wr	dg	ck	tch		
bb	cc	dd	ff	gg	hh	kk	ll	mm
nn	pp	rr	ss	tt	ww	vv	zz	

Section 2: Copywork

Copy the passage and mark all the consonant chunks.

He worked and sang

H

from morn till night,

f

No lark more happy

N

than he.

t

1. Read the rhyme to your student.

2. Read it together slowly. Have the student point to each word as you read.

3. Have your student look for and mark all the **consonant chunks** in blue. Continue to give as much help as is needed.

There once was a jolly miller

Who lived on the river Dee.

He worked and sang from morn till night,

No lark more happy than he.

Consonant Chunks

ch	gh	ph	sh	th	wh		
gn	kn	qu	wr	dg	ck	tch	
bb	cc	dd	ff	gg	hh	kk	ll	mm
nn	pp	rr	ss	tt	ww	vv	zz

Jack and Jill

Copy the passage and mark all the consonant chunks.

There once was

a jolly miller

Who lived on

the river Dee.

1. Read the rhyme to your student.

2. Read it together slowly. Have the student point to each word as you read.

3. Have your student look for and mark all the **consonant chunks** in blue. Continue to give as much help as is needed.

There once was a jolly miller

Who lived on the river Dee.

He worked and sang from morn till night,

No lark more happy than he.

Consonant Chunks

ch	gh	ph	sh	th	wh		
gn	kn	qu	wr	dg	ck	tch	
bb	cc	dd	ff	gg	hh	kk	ll	mm
nn	pp	rr	ss	tt	ww	vv	zz

Draw a picture of the rhyme or write your own story. Be creative and have fun.

1. Read the rhyme to your student.

2. Read it together slowly. Have the student point to each word as you read.

3. Have your student look for and mark all the **consonant chunks** in blue. Continue to give as much help as is needed.

There once was a jolly miller

Who lived on the river Dee.

He worked and sang from morn till night,

No lark more happy than he.

Consonant Chunks

ch	gh	ph	sh	th	wh	
gn	kn	qu	wr	dg	ck	tch
bb	cc	dd	ff	gg	hh	kk	ll	mm
nn	pp	rr	ss	tt	ww	vv	zz

Write this week's rhyme from dictation. Take your time. Ask for help if you need it.

There

Who

He

No

I spelled _____ words correctly.   **93**

28A
Section 1: Consonant Chunks, Endings

1. Read the rhyme to your student.

2. Read it together slowly. Have the student point to each word as you read.

3. Have your student look for and mark all the **consonant chunks** in blue. Together, find and mark the **endings** in pink or red.

Jenny Wren was slowly flying

Over the hills sadly crying,

"Have you seen my lovely locket?

I've searched, and I cannot find it."

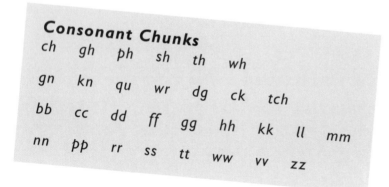

Consonant Chunks

ch	gh	ph	sh	th	wh
gn	kn	qu	wr	dg	ck	tch
bb	cc	dd	ff	gg	hh	kk	ll	mm
nn	pp	rr	ss	tt	ww	vv	zz

Endings
-ed -es -ful -ing -ly

Jack and Jill

Copy the passage and mark all the consonant chunks and endings using the correct colors.

Jenny   Wren

Jenny

was   slowly   flying

was

Over   the   hills

Over

sadly   crying,

sadly

1. Read the rhyme to your student.

2. Read it together slowly. Have the student point to each word as you read.

3. Have your student look for and mark all the **consonant chunks** in blue. Together, find and mark the **endings** in pink or red.

Jenny Wren was slowly flying

Over the hills sadly crying,

"Have you seen my lovely locket?

I've searched, and I cannot find it."

Consonant Chunks

ch	gh	ph	sh	th	wh
gn	kn	qu	wr	dg	ck	tch
bb	cc	dd	ff	gg	hh	kk	ll	mm
nn	pp	rr	ss	tt	ww	vv	zz

Endings
-ed   -es   -ful   -ing   -ly

Copy the passage and mark all the consonant chunks and endings using the correct colors.

"Have you seen

"H

my lovely locket?

m

I've searched, and

I

I cannot find it."

I

1. Read the rhyme to your student.

2. Read it together slowly. Have the student point to each word as you read.

3. Have your student look for and mark all the <u>**consonant chunks**</u> in blue. Together, find and mark the <u>**endings**</u> in pink or red.

Jenny Wren was slowly flying

Over the hills sadly crying,

"Have you seen my lovely locket?

I've searched, and I cannot find it."

Consonant Chunks

ch	gh	ph	sh	th	wh
gn	kn	qu	wr	dg	ck	tch
bb	cc	dd	ff	gg	hh	kk	ll	mm
nn	pp	rr	ss	tt	ww	vv	zz

Endings
-ed -es -ful -ing -ly

Copy the passage and mark all the consonant chunks and endings using the correct colors.

Jenny   Wren

J

was   slowly   flying

W

Over   the   hills

O

sadly   crying,

S

1. Read the rhyme to your student.

2. Read it together slowly. Have the student point to each word as you read.

3. Have your student look for and mark all the <u>**consonant chunks**</u> in blue. Together, find and mark the <u>**endings**</u> in pink or red.

Jenny Wren was slowly flying

Over the hills sadly crying,

"Have you seen my lovely locket?

I've searched, and I cannot find it."

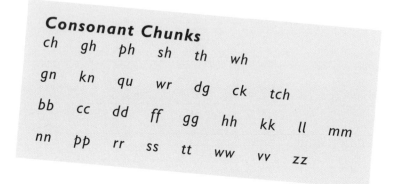

Consonant Chunks

ch	gh	ph	sh	th	wh			
gn	kn	qu	wr	dg	ck	tch		
bb	cc	dd	ff	gg	hh	kk	ll	mm
nn	pp	rr	ss	tt	ww	vv	zz	

Endings
-ed -es -ful -ing -ly

Draw a picture of the rhyme or write your own story. Be creative and have fun.

1. Read the rhyme to your student.

2. Read it together slowly. Have the student point to each word as you read.

3. Have your student look for and mark all the <u>consonant chunks</u> in blue. Together, find and mark the <u>endings</u> in pink or red.

Jenny Wren was slowly flying

Over the hills sadly crying,

"Have you seen my lovely locket?

I've searched, and I cannot find it."

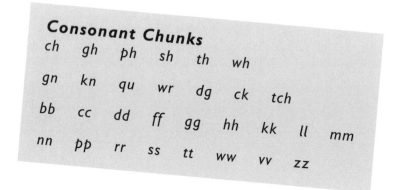

Consonant Chunks

ch	gh	ph	sh	th	wh
gn	kn	qu	wr	dg	ck	tch
bb	cc	dd	ff	gg	hh	kk	ll	mm
nn	pp	rr	ss	tt	ww	vv	zz

Endings
-ed   -es   -ful   -ing   -ly

Section 2: Dictation

Write this week's rhyme from dictation. Take your time. Ask for help if you need it.

Jenny

Over

"Have

I've

29A

Section 1: Consonant Chunks, Tricky y Guy

1. Read the rhyme to your student.

2. Read it together slowly. Have the student point to each word as you read.

3. Have your student look for and mark all the **consonant chunks** in blue. Together, find examples of **Tricky *y* Guy** and mark them in green.

Hickory, dickory, dock,

The mouse ran up the clock.

The clock struck one.

The mouse ran down.

Hickory, dickory, dock.

Consonant Chunks

ch	gh	ph	sh	th	wh
gn	kn	qu	wr	dg	ck	tch
bb	cc	dd	ff	gg	hh	kk	ll	mm
nn	pp	rr	ss	tt	ww	vv	zz

Copy the passage and mark all the consonant chunks and each Tricky *y* Guy.

Hickory, dickory, dock,

Hickory,

The mouse ran

The

up the clock.

up

The clock struck one.

The

1. Read the rhyme to your student.

2. Read it together slowly. Have the student point to each word as you read.

3. Have your student look for and mark all the **consonant chunks** in blue. Together, find examples of **Tricky *y* Guy** and mark them in green.

Hickory, dickory, dock,

The mouse ran up the clock.

The clock struck one.

The mouse ran down.

Hickory, dickory, dock.

Consonant Chunks

ch	gh	ph	sh	th	wh		
gn	kn	qu	wr	dg	ck	tch	
bb	cc	dd	ff	gg	hh	kk	ll	mm
nn	pp	rr	ss	tt	ww	vv	zz

Jack and Jill

Copy the passage and mark all the consonant chunks and each Tricky *y* Guy.

Hickory, dickory, dock,

H

The clock struck one.

T

The mouse ran down.

T

Hickory, dickory, dock.

H

1. Read the rhyme to your student.

2. Read it together slowly. Have the student point to each word as you read.

3. Have your student look for and mark all the **consonant chunks** in blue. Together, find examples of **Tricky *y* Guy** and mark them in green.

Hickory, dickory, dock,

The mouse ran up the clock.

The clock struck one.

The mouse ran down.

Hickory, dickory, dock.

Consonant Chunks

ch	gh	ph	sh	th	wh
gn	kn	qu	wr	dg	ck	tch
bb	cc	dd	ff	gg	hh	kk	ll	mm
nn	pp	rr	ss	tt	ww	vv	zz

Copy the passage and mark all the consonant chunks and each Tricky *y* Guy.

Hickory, dickory, dock,

H

The mouse ran

T

up the clock.

u

The clock struck one.

T

1. Read the rhyme to your student.

2. Read it together slowly. Have the student point to each word as you read.

3. Have your student look for and mark all the <u>consonant chunks</u> in blue. Together, find examples of **Tricky *y* Guy** and mark them in green.

Hickory, dickory, dock,

The mouse ran up the clock.

The clock struck one.

The mouse ran down.

Hickory, dickory, dock.

Consonant Chunks

ch	gh	ph	sh	th	wh		
gn	kn	qu	wr	dg	ck	tch	
bb	cc	dd	ff	gg	hh	kk	ll	mm
nn	pp	rr	ss	tt	ww	vv	zz

Section 2: No Rule Day

Draw a picture of the rhyme or write your own story. Be creative and have fun.

29E
Section 1: Consonant Chunks, Tricky y Guy

1. Read the rhyme to your student.

2. Read it together slowly. Have the student point to each word as you read.

3. Have your student look for and mark all the **consonant chunks** in blue. Together, find examples of **Tricky y Guy** and mark them in green.

Hickory, dickory, dock,

The mouse ran up the clock.

The clock struck one.

The mouse ran down.

Hickory, dickory, dock.

Consonant Chunks

ch gh ph sh th wh

gn kn qu wr dg ck tch

bb cc dd ff gg hh kk ll mm

nn pp rr ss tt ww vv zz

Write this week's rhyme from dictation. Take your time. Ask for help if you need it.

Hickory,

The

The

The

Hickory,

I spelled _____ words correctly.

1. Read the rhyme to your student.

2. Read it together slowly. Have the student point to each word as you read.

3. Working together, find and mark all the <u>vowel chunks</u> in yellow.
Then find the <u>consonant chunks</u> and mark them in blue.

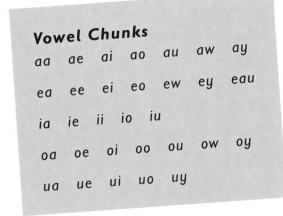

Vowel Chunks

aa	ae	ai	ao	au	aw	ay
ea	ee	ei	eo	ew	ey	eau
ia	ie	ii	io	iu		
oa	oe	oi	oo	ou	ow	oy
ua	ue	ui	uo	uy		

A wise old owl lived in an oak.

The more he saw the less he spoke.

The less he spoke the more he heard.

When he spoke 'twas a thoughtful word.

Consonant Chunks

ch	gh	ph	sh	th	wh					
gn	kn	qu	wr	dg	ck	tch				
bb	cc	dd	ff	gg	hh	kk	ll	mm		
nn	pp	rr	ss	tt	ww	vv	zz			

Copy the passage and mark all the vowel chunks and consonant chunks.

A   wise   old   owl

A

lived   in   an   oak.

lived

The   more   he   saw

The

the   less   he   spoke.

the

30B

Section 1: Vowel and Consonant Chunks

1. Read the rhyme to your student.

2. Read it together slowly. Have the student point to each word as you read.

3. Working together, find and mark all the <u>vowel chunks</u> in yellow.
   Then find the <u>consonant chunks</u> and mark them in blue.

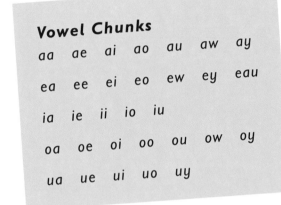

Vowel Chunks

aa	ae	ai	ao	au	aw	ay
ea	ee	ei	eo	ew	ey	eau
ia	ie	ii	io	iu		
oa	oe	oi	oo	ou	ow	oy
ua	ue	ui	uo	uy		

A wise old owl lived in an oak.

The more he saw the less he spoke.

The less he spoke the more he heard.

When he spoke 'twas a thoughtful word.

Consonant Chunks

ch	gh	ph	sh	th	wh
gn	kn	qu	wr	dg	ck	tch
bb	cc	dd	ff	gg	hh	kk	ll	mm
nn	pp	rr	ss	tt	ww	vv	zz

116

Jack and Jill

Copy the passage and mark all the vowel chunks and consonant chunks.

The less he spoke

T

the more he heard.

t

When he spoke

W

'twas a thoughtful word.

't

30C
Section 1: Vowel and Consonant Chunks

1. Read the rhyme to your student.

2. Read it together slowly. Have the student point to each word as you read.

3. Working together, find and mark all the **vowel chunks** in yellow.
   Then find the **consonant chunks** and mark them in blue.

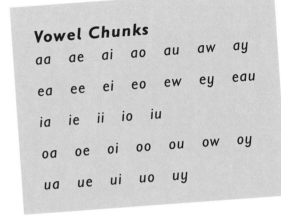

Vowel Chunks

aa	ae	ai	ao	au	aw	ay
ea	ee	ei	eo	ew	ey	eau
ia	ie	ii	io	iu		
oa	oe	oi	oo	ou	ow	oy
ua	ue	ui	uo	uy		

A wise old owl lived in an oak.

The more he saw the less he spoke.

The less he spoke the more he heard.

When he spoke 'twas a thoughtful word.

Consonant Chunks

ch	gh	ph	sh	th	wh	
gn	kn	qu	wr	dg	ck	tch
bb	cc	dd	ff	gg	hh	kk	ll	mm
nn	pp	rr	ss	tt	ww	vv	zz

Jack and Jill

Copy the passage and mark all the vowel chunks and consonant chunks.

A wise old owl

A

lived in an oak.

l

The more he saw

T

the less he spoke.

t

30D Section 1: Vowel and Consonant Chunks

1. Read the rhyme to your student.

2. Read it together slowly. Have the student point to each word as you read.

3. Working together, find and mark all the **vowel chunks** in yellow.
   Then find the **consonant chunks** and mark them in blue.

A wise old owl lived in an oak.

The more he saw the less he spoke.

The less he spoke the more he heard.

When he spoke 'twas a thoughtful word.

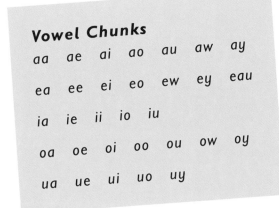

Vowel Chunks

aa	ae	ai	ao	au	aw	ay
ea	ee	ei	eo	ew	ey	eau
ia	ie	ii	io	iu		
oa	oe	oi	oo	ou	ow	oy
ua	ue	ui	uo	uy		

Consonant Chunks

ch	gh	ph	sh	th	wh	
gn	kn	qu	wr	dg	ck	tch
bb	cc	dd	ff	gg	hh	kk	ll	mm
nn	pp	rr	ss	tt	ww	vv	zz

Jack and Jill

Draw a picture of the rhyme or write your own story. Be creative and have fun.

30E

Section 1: Vowel and Consonant Chunks

1. Read the rhyme to your student.

2. Read it together slowly. Have the student point to each word as you read.

3. Working together, find and mark all the **vowel chunks** in yellow.
   Then find the **consonant chunks** and mark them in blue.

A wise old owl lived in an oak.

The more he saw the less he spoke.

The less he spoke the more he heard.

When he spoke 'twas a thoughtful word.

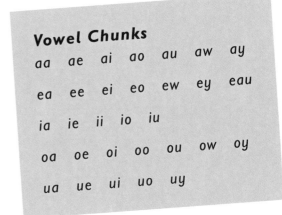

Vowel Chunks

aa	ae	ai	ao	au	aw	ay
ea	ee	ei	eo	ew	ey	eau
ia	ie	ii	io	iu		
oa	oe	oi	oo	ou	ow	oy
ua	ue	ui	uo	uy		

Consonant Chunks

ch	gh	ph	sh	th	wh	
gn	kn	qu	wr	dg	ck	tch
bb	cc	dd	ff	gg	hh	kk	ll	mm
nn	pp	rr	ss	tt	ww	vv	zz

Jack and Jill

Write this week's rhyme from dictation. Take your time. Ask for help if you need it.

A

The

The

When

I spelled _____ words correctly.

1. Read the rhyme to your student.

2. Read it together slowly. Have the student point to each word as you read.

3. Working together, first find and mark all the **consonant chunks** in blue. Then find examples of **silent _e_** and **silent _b_** that are not part of other chunks. Mark the silent letters in orange.

This old man, he played one,

He played knick-knack on his thumb.

With a knick-knack paddy whack,

Give the dog a bone.

This old man came rolling home!

Consonant Chunks

ch	gh	ph	sh	th	wh
gn	kn	qu	wr	dg	ck	tch
bb	cc	dd	ff	gg	hh	kk	ll	mm
nn	pp	rr	ss	tt	ww	vv	zz

Copy the passage. Mark all the consonant chunks and silent letters.

This old man, he

This

played one,

played

He played knick-knack

He

on his thumb.

on

31B Section 1: Consonant Chunks, Silent Letters

1. Read the rhyme to your student.

2. Read it together slowly. Have the student point to each word as you read.

3. Working together, first find and mark all the <u>consonant chunks</u> in blue. Then find examples of **silent _e_** and **silent _b_** that are not part of other chunks. Mark the silent letters in orange.

This old man, he played one,

He played knick-knack on his thumb.

With a knick-knack paddy whack,

Give the dog a bone.

This old man came rolling home!

Consonant Chunks

ch	gh	ph	sh	th	wh
gn	kn	qu	wr	dg	ck	tch
bb	cc	dd	ff	gg	hh	kk	ll	mm
nn	pp	rr	ss	tt	ww	vv	zz

Section 2: Copywork

Copy the passage. Mark all the consonant chunks and silent letters.

With a knick-knack

W

paddy whack,

P

Give the dog a bone.

G

This old man came

T

1. Read the rhyme to your student.

2. Read it together slowly. Have the student point to each word as you read.

3. Working together, first find and mark all the <u>**consonant chunks**</u> in blue. Then find examples of **silent _e_** and **silent _b_** that are not part of other chunks. Mark the silent letters in orange.

This old man, he played one,

He played knick-knack on his thumb.

With a knick-knack paddy whack,

Give the dog a bone.

This old man came rolling home!

Consonant Chunks

ch	gh	ph	sh	th	wh
gn	kn	qu	wr	dg	ck	tch
bb	cc	dd	ff	gg	hh	kk	ll	mm
nn	pp	rr	ss	tt	ww	vv	zz

Copy the passage. Mark all the consonant chunks and silent letters.

knick-knack paddy whack,

k

Give the dog a bone.

G

This old man came

T

rolling home!

r

31D

Section 1: Consonant Chunks, Silent Letters

1. Read the rhyme to your student.

2. Read it together slowly. Have the student point to each word as you read.

3. Working together, first find and mark all the **consonant chunks** in blue. Then find examples of **silent *e*** and **silent *b*** that are not part of other chunks. Mark the silent letters in orange.

This old man, he played one,

He played knick-knack on his thumb.

With a knick-knack paddy whack,

Give the dog a bone.

This old man came rolling home!

Consonant Chunks

ch	gh	ph	sh	th	wh
gn	kn	qu	wr	dg	ck	tch
bb	cc	dd	ff	gg	hh	kk	ll	mm
nn	pp	rr	ss	tt	ww	vv	zz

Draw a picture of the rhyme or write your own story. Be creative and have fun.

1. Read the rhyme to your student.

2. Read it together slowly. Have the student point to each word as you read.

3. Working together, first find and mark all the **consonant chunks** in blue. Then find examples of **silent _e_** and **silent _b_** that are not part of other chunks. Mark the silent letters in orange.

This old man, he played one,

He played knick-knack on his thumb.

With a knick-knack paddy whack,

Give the dog a bone.

This old man came rolling home!

Consonant Chunks

ch	gh	ph	sh	th	wh
gn	kn	qu	wr	dg	ck	tch
bb	cc	dd	ff	gg	hh	kk	ll	mm
nn	pp	rr	ss	tt	ww	vv	zz

Write this week's rhyme from dictation. Take your time. Ask for help if you need it.

This

He

With

Give

This

I spelled _____ words correctly.

32A
Section 1: Consonant Chunks, Silent Letters

1. Read the rhyme to your student.

2. Read it together slowly. Have the student point to each word as you read.

3. Working together, first find and mark all the **consonant chunks** in blue. Then find examples of **silent _e_** and mark them in orange.

One, two, buckle my shoe.

Three, four, shut the door.

Five, six, pick up sticks.

Seven, eight, lay them straight.

Nine, ten, big fat hen.

Consonant Chunks

ch	gh	ph	sh	th	wh			
gn	kn	qu	wr	dg	ck	tch		
bb	cc	dd	ff	gg	hh	kk	ll	mm
nn	pp	rr	ss	tt	ww	vv	zz	

Copy the passage. Mark all the consonant chunks and each silent *e*.

One, two, buckle my shoe.

One

Three, four, shut the door.

Three

Five, six, pick up sticks.

Five

Seven, eight,

Seven

32B

1. Read the rhyme to your student.

2. Read it together slowly. Have the student point to each word as you read.

3. Working together, first find and mark all the **consonant chunks** in blue. Then find examples of **silent _e_** and mark them in orange.

One, two, buckle my shoe.

Three, four, shut the door.

Five, six, pick up sticks.

Seven, eight, lay them straight.

Nine, ten, big fat hen.

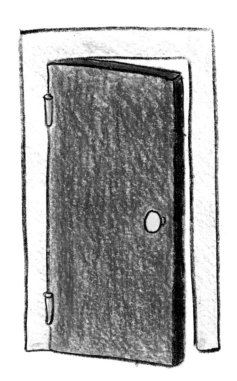

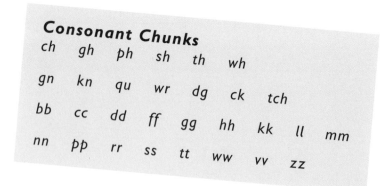

Consonant Chunks

ch   gh   ph   sh   th   wh

gn   kn   qu   wr   dg   ck   tch

bb   cc   dd   ff   gg   hh   kk   ll   mm

nn   pp   rr   ss   tt   ww   vv   zz

Jack and Jill

Section 2: Copywork

Copy the passage. Mark all the consonant chunks and each silent *e*.

Five, six, pick up sticks.

F

Seven, eight,

S

lay them straight.

l

Nine, ten, big fat hen.

N

Jack and Jill   32B

1. Read the rhyme to your student.

2. Read it together slowly. Have the student point to each word as you read.

3. Working together, first find and mark all the **consonant chunks** in blue. Then find examples of **silent _e_** and mark them in orange.

One, two, buckle my shoe.

Three, four, shut the door.

Five, six, pick up sticks.

Seven, eight, lay them straight.

Nine, ten, big fat hen.

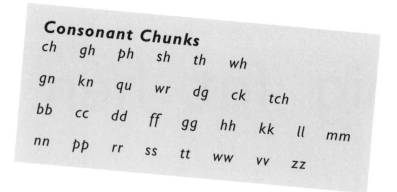

Consonant Chunks

ch	gh	ph	sh	th	wh			
gn	kn	qu	wr	dg	ck	tch		
bb	cc	dd	ff	gg	hh	kk	ll	mm
nn	pp	rr	ss	tt	ww	vv	zz	

Copy the passage. Mark all the consonant chunks and each silent *e*.

One, two, buckle my shoe.

O

Three, four, shut the door.

T

Five, six, pick up sticks.

F

Seven, eight,

S

32D

Section 1: Consonant Chunks, Silent Letters

1. Read the rhyme to your student.

2. Read it together slowly. Have the student point to each word as you read.

3. Working together, first find and mark all the **consonant chunks** in blue. Then find examples of **silent _e_** and mark them in orange.

One, two, buckle my shoe.

Three, four, shut the door.

Five, six, pick up sticks.

Seven, eight, lay them straight.

Nine, ten, big fat hen.

Consonant Chunks

ch	gh	ph	sh	th	wh		
gn	kn	qu	wr	dg	ck	tch	
bb	cc	dd	ff	gg	hh	kk	ll	mm
nn	pp	rr	ss	tt	ww	vv	zz

Draw a picture of the rhyme or write your own story. Be creative and have fun.

1. Read the rhyme to your student.

2. Read it together slowly. Have the student point to each word as you read.

3. Working together, first find and mark all the **consonant chunks** in blue. Then find examples of **silent _e_** and mark them in orange.

One, two, buckle my shoe.

Three, four, shut the door.

Five, six, pick up sticks.

Seven, eight, lay them straight.

Nine, ten, big fat hen.

Consonant Chunks

ch gh ph sh th wh

gn kn qu wr dg ck tch

bb cc dd ff gg hh kk ll mm

nn pp rr ss tt ww vv zz

Write this week's rhyme from dictation. Take your time. Ask for help if you need it.

One,

Three,

Five,

Seven,

Nine,

I spelled _____ words correctly.

33A
Section 1: Consonant Chunks, Silent Letters, Tricky y Guy

1. Read the rhyme to your student and then read it together slowly.

2. This week your student will be marking three different kinds of chunks. Be sure to give all the help that is needed.

3. Have the student mark all the **consonant chunks** in blue. Then find the **silent letters** and mark them in orange. Finally, mark each **Tricky y Guy** in green.

This little piggy went to market.

This little piggy stayed home.

This little piggy had roast beef.

This little piggy had none.

This little piggy cried,

"Wee, wee, wee, wee, wee,"

All the way home.

Consonant Chunks

ch	gh	ph	sh	th	wh
gn	kn	qu	wr	dg	ck	tch
bb	cc	dd	ff	gg	hh	kk	ll	mm
nn	pp	rr	ss	tt	ww	vv	zz

Copy and chunk the passage, marking the same chunks and letters that you marked on the previous page.

This little piggy

This

went to market.

went

This little piggy

This

stayed home.

stayed

33B

Section 1: Consonant Chunks, Silent Letters, Tricky y Guy

1. Read the rhyme to your student and then read it together slowly.

2. This week your student will be marking three different kinds of chunks. Be sure to give all the help that is needed.

3. Have the student mark all the **consonant chunks** in blue. Then find the **silent letters** and mark them in orange. Finally, mark each **Tricky y Guy** in green.

This little piggy went to market.

This little piggy stayed home.

This little piggy had roast beef.

This little piggy had none.

This little piggy cried,

"Wee, wee, wee, wee, wee,"

All the way home.

Consonant Chunks					
ch	gh	ph	sh	th	wh
gn	kn	qu	wr	dg	ck	tch
bb	cc	dd	ff	gg	hh	kk	ll	mm
nn	pp	rr	ss	tt	ww	vv	zz

Jack and Jill

Copy and chunk the passage, marking the same chunks and letters that you marked on the previous page.

This   little   piggy   had

T

roast   beef.

r

This   little   piggy

T

had   none.

h

1. Read the rhyme to your student and then read it together slowly.

2. This week your student will be marking three different kinds of chunks. Be sure to give all the help that is needed.

3. Have the student mark all the **consonant chunks** in blue. Then find the <u>silent letters</u> and mark them in orange. Finally, mark each **Tricky *y* Guy** in green.

This little piggy went to market.

This little piggy stayed home.

This little piggy had roast beef.

This little piggy had none.

This little piggy cried,

"Wee, wee, wee, wee, wee,"

All the way home.

Consonant Chunks

ch	gh	ph	sh	th	wh		
gn	kn	qu	wr	dg	ck	tch	
bb	cc	dd	ff	gg	hh	kk	ll	mm
nn	pp	rr	ss	tt	ww	vv	zz	

Section 2: Copywork

Copy and chunk the passage, marking the same chunks and letters that you marked on the previous page.

This little piggy cried,

T

"Wee, wee, wee,

"W

wee, wee,"

W

All the way home.

A

Jack and Jill   33C

149

1. Read the rhyme to your student and then read it together slowly.

2. This week your student will be marking three different kinds of chunks. Be sure to give all the help that is needed.

3. Have the student mark all the **consonant chunks** in blue. Then find the **silent letters** and mark them in orange. Finally, mark each **Tricky y Guy** in green.

This little piggy went to market.

This little piggy stayed home.

This little piggy had roast beef.

This little piggy had none.

This little piggy cried,

"Wee, wee, wee, wee, wee,"

All the way home.

Consonant Chunks

ch	gh	ph	sh	th	wh
gn	kn	qu	wr	dg	ck	tch
bb	cc	dd	ff	gg	hh	kk	ll	mm
nn	pp	rr	ss	tt	ww	vv	zz

Draw a picture of the rhyme or write your own story. Be creative and have fun.

Section 1: Consonant Chunks, Silent Letters, Tricky y Guy

1. Read the rhyme to your student and then read it together slowly.

2. This week your student will be marking three different kinds of chunks. Be sure to give all the help that is needed.

3. Have the student mark all the **consonant chunks** in blue. Then find the **silent letters** and mark them in orange. Finally, mark each **Tricky y Guy** in green.

This little piggy went to market.

This little piggy stayed home.

This little piggy had roast beef.

This little piggy had none.

This little piggy cried,

"Wee, wee, wee, wee, wee,"

All the way home.

Consonant Chunks

ch gh ph sh th wh

gn kn qu wr dg ck tch

bb cc dd ff gg hh kk ll mm

nn pp rr ss tt ww vv zz

Turn the page to write this week's story from dictation.

Write this week's rhyme from dictation. Take your time. Ask for help if you need it.

This

This

This

This

This

"Wee,

All

I spelled _____ words correctly.

1. Read the rhyme to your student and then read it together slowly.

2. Encourage your student to work independently if possible. Always check the chunking in Section 1 so that it can be used as a guide when chunking the copywork page.

3. Have the student mark all the **vowel chunks** in yellow and each **Tricky *y* Guy** in green.

Humpty Dumpty sat on a wall.

Humpty Dumpty had a great fall.

All the king's horses

And all the king's men

Couldn't put Humpty together again.

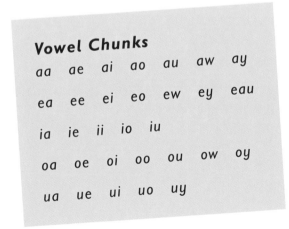

Vowel Chunks

aa	ae	ai	ao	au	aw	ay
ea	ee	ei	eo	ew	ey	eau
ia	ie	ii	io	iu		
oa	oe	oi	oo	ou	ow	oy
ua	ue	ui	uo	uy		

Copy and chunk the passage, marking the same chunks and letters that you marked on the previous page.

Humpty Dumpty

H

sat on a wall.

s

Humpty Dumpty

H

had a great fall.

h

34B

1. Read the rhyme to your student and then read it together slowly.

2. Encourage your student to work independently if possible. Always check the chunking in Section 1 so that it can be used as a guide when chunking the copywork page.

3. Have the student mark all the **vowel chunks** in yellow and each **Tricky *y* Guy** in green.

Humpty Dumpty sat on a wall.

Humpty Dumpty had a great fall.

All the king's horses

And all the king's men

Couldn't put Humpty together again.

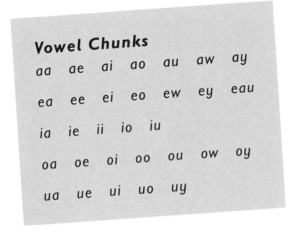

Vowel Chunks

aa	ae	ai	ao	au	aw	ay
ea	ee	ei	eo	ew	ey	eau
ia	ie	ii	io	iu		
oa	oe	oi	oo	ou	ow	oy
ua	ue	ui	uo	uy		

Section 2: Copywork

Copy and chunk the passage, marking the same chunks and letters that you marked on the previous page.

All the king's horses

A

And all the king's men

A

Couldn't put Humpty

C

together again.

t

1. Read the rhyme to your student and then read it together slowly.

2. Encourage your student to work independently if possible. Always check the chunking in Section 1 so that it can be used as a guide when chunking the copywork page.

3. Have the student mark all the **vowel chunks** in yellow and each **Tricky *y* Guy** in green.

Humpty Dumpty sat on a wall.

Humpty Dumpty had a great fall.

All the king's horses

And all the king's men

Couldn't put Humpty together again.

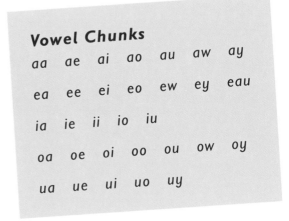

Vowel Chunks

aa	ae	ai	ao	au	aw	ay
ea	ee	ei	eo	ew	ey	eau
ia	ie	ii	io	iu		
oa	oe	oi	oo	ou	ow	oy
ua	ue	ui	uo	uy		

Copy and chunk the passage, marking the same chunks and letters that you marked on the previous page.

Humpty   Dumpty

H

sat   on   a   wall.

s

Humpty   Dumpty

H

had   a   great   fall.

h

1. Read the rhyme to your student and then read it together slowly.

2. Encourage your student to work independently if possible. Always check the chunking in Section 1 so that it can be used as a guide when chunking the copywork page.

3. Have the student mark all the **vowel chunks** in yellow and each **Tricky *y* Guy** in green.

Humpty Dumpty sat on a wall.

Humpty Dumpty had a great fall.

All the king's horses

And all the king's men

Couldn't put Humpty together again.

Vowel Chunks

aa	ae	ai	ao	au	aw	ay
ea	ee	ei	eo	ew	ey	eau
ia	ie	ii	io	iu		
oa	oe	oi	oo	ou	ow	oy
ua	ue	ui	uo	uy		

Draw a picture of the rhyme or write your own story. Be creative and have fun.

34E
Section 1: Vowel Chunks, Tricky y Guy

1. Read the rhyme to your student and then read it together slowly.

2. Encourage your student to work independently if possible. Always check the chunking in Section 1 so that it can be used as a guide when chunking the copywork page.

3. Have the student mark all the **vowel chunks** in yellow and each **Tricky y Guy** in green.

Humpty Dumpty sat on a wall.

Humpty Dumpty had a great fall.

All the king's horses

And all the king's men

Couldn't put Humpty together again.

Vowel Chunks

aa	ae	ai	ao	au	aw	ay
ea	ee	ei	eo	ew	ey	eau
ia	ie	ii	io	iu		
oa	oe	oi	oo	ou	ow	oy
ua	ue	ui	uo	uy		

164

Jack and Jill

Turn the page to write this week's story from dictation.

Write this week's rhyme from dictation. Take your time. Ask for help if you need it.

Humpty

Humpty

All

And

Couldn't

1. Read the rhyme to your student and then read it together slowly.

2. Help the student mark **vowel chunks** in yellow, each **Tricky *y* Guy** in green, and <u>endings</u> in pink or red.

There was an old lady who swallowed a fly.

I don't know why she swallowed the fly.

I guess she'll die.

There was an old lady who swallowed a spider

That wiggled and jiggled and tickled inside her.

She swallowed the spider to catch the fly.

I don't know why she swallowed the fly.

I guess she'll die.

Vowel Chunks

aa	ae	ai	ao	au	aw	ay
ea	ee	ei	eo	ew	ey	eau
ia	ie	ii	io	iu		
oa	oe	oi	oo	ou	ow	oy
ua	ue	ui	uo	uy		

Endings
-ed -es -ful -ing -ly

Jack and Jill

Copy and chunk the passage, marking the same chunks and letters that you marked on the previous page.

There was an old lady

T

who swallowed a fly.

W

I don't know why

I

she swallowed the fly.

S

Section 1: Vowel Chunks, Tricky y Guy, Endings

1. Read the rhyme to your student and then read it together slowly.

2. Help the student mark **vowel chunks** in yellow, each **Tricky y Guy** in green, and **endings** in pink or red.

There was an old lady who swallowed a fly.

I don't know why she swallowed the fly.

I guess she'll die.

There was an old lady who swallowed a spider

That wiggled and jiggled and tickled inside her.

She swallowed the spider to catch the fly.

I don't know why she swallowed the fly.

I guess she'll die.

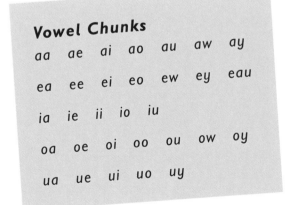

Vowel Chunks

aa   ae   ai   ao   au   aw   ay

ea   ee   ei   eo   ew   ey   eau

ia   ie   ii   io   iu

oa   oe   oi   oo   ou   ow   oy

ua   ue   ui   uo   uy

Endings
-ed   -es   -ful   -ing   -ly

Copy and chunk the passage, marking the same chunks and letters that you marked on the previous page.

There was an old lady

T

who swallowed a spider

W

That wiggled and jiggled

T

and tickled inside her.

a

1. Read the rhyme to your student and then read it together slowly.

2. Help the student mark **vowel chunks** in yellow, each **Tricky _y_ Guy** in green, and <u>endings</u> in pink or red.

There was an old lady who swallowed a fly.

I don't know why she swallowed the fly.

I guess she'll die.

There was an old lady who swallowed a spider

That wiggled and jiggled and tickled inside her.

She swallowed the spider to catch the fly.

I don't know why she swallowed the fly.

I guess she'll die.

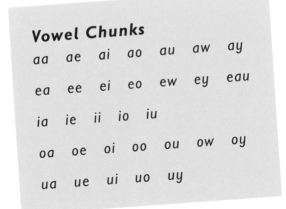

Vowel Chunks

aa	ae	ai	ao	au	aw	ay
ea	ee	ei	eo	ew	ey	eau
ia	ie	ii	io	iu		
oa	oe	oi	oo	ou	ow	oy
ua	ue	ui	uo	uy		

Endings
-ed -es -ful -ing -ly

Copy and chunk the passage, marking all the same letters that you marked on the previous page.

She swallowed the

S

spider to catch the fly.

s

I don't know why

I

she swallowed the fly.

s

1. Read the rhyme to your student and then read it together slowly.

2. Help the student mark <u>vowel chunks</u> in yellow, each <u>**Tricky *y* Guy**</u> in green, and <u>endings</u> in pink or red.

There was an old lady who swallowed a fly.

I don't know why she swallowed the fly.

I guess she'll die.

There was an old lady who swallowed a spider

That wiggled and jiggled and tickled inside her.

She swallowed the spider to catch the fly.

I don't know why she swallowed the fly.

I guess she'll die.

Vowel Chunks

aa ae ai ao au aw ay

ea ee ei eo ew ey eau

ia ie ii io iu

oa oe oi oo ou ow oy

ua ue ui uo uy

Endings
-ed -es -ful -ing -ly

Draw a picture of the rhyme or write your own story. Be creative and have fun.

1. Read the rhyme to your student and then read it together slowly.

2. Help the student mark **vowel chunks** in yellow, each **Tricky _y_ Guy** in green, and <u>endings</u> with pink or red.

There was an old lady who swallowed a fly.

I don't know why she swallowed the fly.

I guess she'll die.

There was an old lady who swallowed a spider

That wiggled and jiggled and tickled inside her.

She swallowed the spider to catch the fly.

I don't know why she swallowed the fly.

I guess she'll die.

Endings
-ed -es -ful -ing -ly

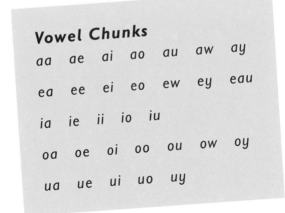

Vowel Chunks

aa ae ai ao au aw ay

ea ee ei eo ew ey eau

ia ie ii io iu

oa oe oi oo ou ow oy

ua ue ui uo uy

Jack and Jill

Turn the page to write this week's story from dictation.

Write this week's rhyme from dictation. Take your time. Ask for help if you need it.

There

Jack and Jill

I spelled _____ words correctly.

1. Read the rhyme to your student and then read it together slowly.

2. Help the student mark **consonant chunks** in blue, **Bossy *r* chunks** in purple, and **silent letters** in orange.

3. When doing copywork or dictation, the student does not need to include the "EIEIO" refrain.

Old MacDonald had a farm, E I E I O.

And on his farm he had some ducks, E I E I O.

With a quack, quack here and a quack, quack there,

Here a quack, there a quack, everywhere a quack, quack.

Old MacDonald had a farm, E I E I O!

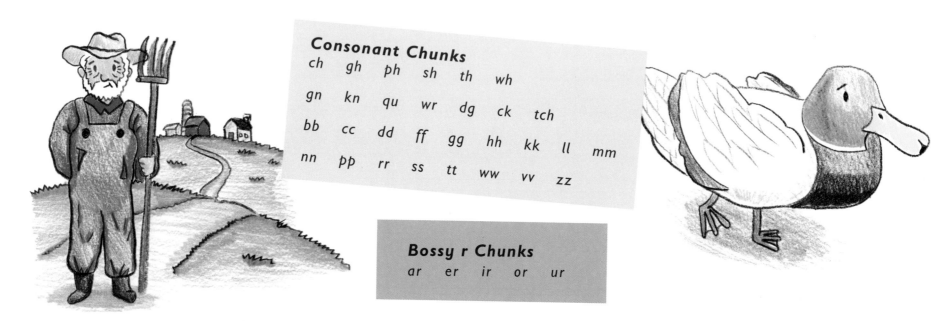

Consonant Chunks

ch	gh	ph	sh	th	wh
gn	kn	qu	wr	dg	ck	tch
bb	cc	dd	ff	gg	hh	kk	ll	mm
nn	pp	rr	ss	tt	ww	vv	zz

Bossy r Chunks

ar er ir or ur

Copy and chunk the passage, marking the same chunks and letters that you marked on the previous page.

Old MacDonald had a farm.

O

And on his farm

A

he had some ducks.

h

With a quack, quack here

W

1. Read the rhyme to your student and then read it together slowly.

2. Help the student mark **consonant chunks** in blue, **Bossy *r* chunks** in purple, and **silent letters** in orange.

Old MacDonald had a farm, E I E I O.

And on his farm he had some chickens, E I E I O.

With a cluck, cluck here and a cluck, cluck there,

Here a cluck, there a cluck, everywhere a cluck, cluck.

Old MacDonald had a farm, E I E I O!

Consonant Chunks

ch	gh	ph	sh	th	wh
gn	kn	qu	wr	dg	ck	tch
bb	cc	dd	ff	gg	hh	kk	ll	mm
nn	pp	rr	ss	tt	ww	vv	zz

Bossy r Chunks

ar   er   ir   or   ur

Copy and chunk the passage, marking the same chunks and letters that you marked on the previous page.

And on his farm

A

he had some chickens.

h

With a cluck, cluck here

W

And a cluck, cluck there,

A

1. Read the rhyme to your student and then read it together slowly.

2. Help the student mark **consonant chunks** in blue, **Bossy *r* chunks** in purple, and **silent letters** in orange.

Old MacDonald had a farm, E I E I O.

And on his farm he had some cows, E I E I O.

With a moo, moo here and a moo, moo there,

Here a moo, there a moo, everywhere a moo, moo.

Old MacDonald had a farm, E I E I O!

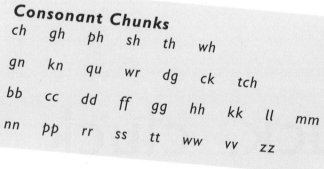

Consonant Chunks

ch	gh	ph	sh	th	wh			
gn	kn	qu	wr	dg	ck	tch		
bb	cc	dd	ff	gg	hh	kk	ll	mm
nn	pp	rr	ss	tt	ww	vv	zz	

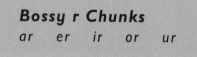

Bossy r Chunks

ar   er   ir   or   ur

Copy and chunk the passage, marking the same chunks and letters that you marked on the previous page.

And on his farm

A

he had some cows.

h

With a moo, moo here

W

And a moo, moo there,

A

Section 1: Consonant Chunks, Bossy *r* Chunks, Silent Letters

1. Read the rhyme to your student and then read it together slowly.

2. Help the student mark **consonant chunks** in blue, **Bossy *r* chunks** in purple, and **silent letters** in orange.

Old MacDonald had a farm, E I E I O.

And on his farm he had some sheep, E I E I O.

With a baa, baa here and a baa, baa there,

Here a baa, there a baa, everywhere a baa, baa.

Old MacDonald had a farm, E I E I O!

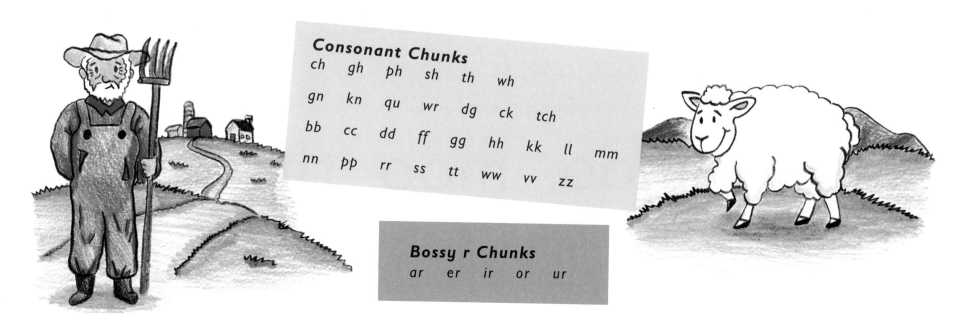

Consonant Chunks

ch gh ph sh th wh

gn kn qu wr dg ck tch

bb cc dd ff gg hh kk ll mm

nn pp rr ss tt ww vv zz

Bossy r Chunks

ar er ir or ur

Section 2: No Rule Day

Draw a picture of the rhyme or write your own story. Be creative and have fun.

1. Read the rhyme to your student and then read it together slowly.

2. Help the student mark **consonant chunks** in blue, **Bossy *r* chunks** in purple, and **silent letters** in orange.

Old MacDonald had a farm, E I E I O.

And on his farm he had a dog, E I E I O.

With a woof, woof here and a woof, woof there,

Here a woof, there a woof, everywhere a woof, woof.

Old MacDonald had a farm, E I E I O!

Consonant Chunks

ch	gh	ph	sh	th	wh	
gn	kn	qu	wr	dg	ck	tch
bb	cc	dd	ff	gg	hh	kk	ll	mm
nn	pp	rr	ss	tt	ww	vv	zz

Bossy r Chunks

ar   er   ir   or   ur

Turn the page to write this week's story from dictation. You need to write only one verse of the poem.

Write this week's rhyme from dictation. Take your time. Ask for help if you need it.

Old

I spelled _____ words correctly.